BUSINESS BEGINNINGS

A Mompreneur's Guide to Launching Your Empire

TAMMY CAPRI

Business Beginnings: A Mompreneurs Guide to Building Your Empire

Copyright © 2024 by Tammy Capri

All rights reserved. No part of this book may be reproduced, transmitted, or stored in whole or in part by any means, including graphic, electronic, or mechanical without the express written consent of the author except in the case of brief quotations embodied in critical articles and reviews.

The information provided in this book, **Business Beginnings: A Mompreneurs Guide to Building Your Empire**, is for general informational purposes only and is not intended to be a substitute for professional advice, whether legal, financial, or otherwise. The author and publisher have made every effort to ensure the accuracy of the information contained within this book as of the date of publication; however, the nature of business and entrepreneurship is continually evolving, and information may become outdated.

The strategies, tips, and stories shared are based on personal experiences and insights, and results may vary based on individual circumstances. Readers are encouraged to consult with appropriate professionals before making any business, financial, or legal decisions.

The author and publisher disclaim any liability or responsibility to any person or entity for any loss, damage, or disruption caused by errors or omissions, whether such errors or omissions result from negligence, accident, or any other cause. This book is sold with the understanding that the author and publisher are not engaged in rendering professional services. If expert assistance is required, the services of a competent professional should be sought.

By reading this book, you acknowledge and agree that the author and publisher are not responsible for your success or failure as a result of the information provided. Your use of any information or materials provided in this book is entirely at your own risk.

Table of Contents

Acknowledgements...9

Introduction..11
    Overview of the Book
    Purpose and Objectives

Chapter 1: Dream Big, Mama...................................14
    Taking the Leap into Mompreneurship
    Finding Your Why

Chapter 2: Finding Your Passion............................19
    Identifying Your Interests and Strengths
    Aligning Passion with Purpose

Chapter 3: Embracing Faith & Finding Purpose.......30
    The Role of Faith in Entrepreneurship
    Discovering Your True Purpose

Chapter 4: Overcoming Self-Doubt........................35
    Recognizing and Addressing Self-Doubt
    Building Confidence and Resilience

Chapter 5: The Freedom 5......................................41
    Exploring E-commerce Excellence
    Service Savvy, Content Creation, and More

Chapter 6: Defining Your Brand.............................48
    Crafting Your Brand Identity
    Building a Strong Online Presence

Chapter 7: Setting SMART Goals..........................55
  Importance of SMART Goals
  Implementing and Achieving Your Goals

Chapter 8: Me vs Time...61
  Time Management Strategies for Mompreneurs
  Balancing Work and Family Life

Chapter 9: From Idea to Reality..............................64
  Developing and Testing Your Ideas
  Creating a Solid Business Plan

Chapter 10: Marketing Magic for Mompreneurs.......72
  Crafting a Winning Marketing Strategy
  Building an Engaging Online Presence

Chapter 11: Scaling & Growing Your Business..........90
  Expanding Your Product Line
  Hiring Help and Staying Motivated

Chapter 12: Get Your Money Right...........................97
  Budgeting and Cash Flow Management
  Understanding Taxes and Financial Planning

Chapter 13: The Heartbeat of Your Business..........105
  Delivering Outstanding Customer Service
  Building Customer Loyalty

Chapter 14: Turning Struggles into Strengths........112
  Overcoming Setbacks and Failures
  Managing Stress and Maintaining Balance

Chapter 15: Building a Legacy.............................121
　Creating Generational Wealth
　Leaving a Lasting Impact

Chapter 16: Embrace Your Journey & Trust in God..129
　Reflections on the Entrepreneurial Journey
　Trusting in God's Plan and Enjoying the Ride

Acknowledgements

First and foremost, I want to give all glory and thanks to God for His unwavering guidance and strength throughout this journey. Without His grace, none of this would be possible.

It's been a long time since my last book was released, and re-entering the book space with something as powerful and helpful as this guide has been a dream come true. This book is more than just words on paper; it's a testament to the growth, challenges, and triumphs that have shaped me into the person I am today.

To my incredible family, thank you for your endless love, patience, and support. Your belief in me has been my anchor, especially during the toughest times. You've given me the strength to pursue my dreams and the courage to share my story with the world.

To everyone who has contributed to making Tammy Capri a better person and brand, I am deeply grateful. From my mentors and coaches to my friends and colleagues, your guidance, feedback, and encouragement have been invaluable. You've helped me learn, grow, and reach new heights.

A special thank you to the amazing community of people who have trusted me to help them through their own trials and tribulations. Your faith in my ability to guide and support you has been both humbling and inspiring. This book is for you – to empower, uplift, and remind you that with faith and hard work, anything is possible.

Finally, to all the readers who have picked up this book, thank you for allowing me to be a part of your journey. I hope this guide serves as a beacon of hope, motivation, and practical advice as you build your own empire. Remember, you are capable, you are strong, and you are destined for greatness. Let's make history together.

With heartfelt gratitude,

Tammy Capri

Hey there, fabulous moms!

Welcome to the beginning of an incredible journey. If you're holding this guide, it's because you've got a dream, and let me tell you, dreams are the seeds of greatness. I'm here to help you water that seed, nurture it, and watch it grow into a flourishing business. Whether you're dreaming of opening a boutique, launching an online course, or starting a luxury handbag line (hello, Lecce Capri!), this guide is your road map to success.

When I was a little girl, I used to dream about owning my own hair salon. I imagined doing hair for the stars, creating beautiful styles that would grace red carpets and magazine covers. To my family, it seemed far-fetched. They saw it as just a little girl's fantasy, but dreaming big kept me wanting it anyway. That dream fueled my passion, kept me focused, and ultimately led me down the path of entrepreneurship. It was that vision of a brighter future that drove me to overcome obstacles and seize opportunities, turning my dreams into reality.

Dreaming big is essential because it sets the stage for what you can achieve. It allows you to envision a future beyond your current circumstances and inspires you to work toward something greater. This guide is designed to help you take those big dreams and turn them into reality. It will equip you with the knowledge, tools, and confidence to transform your passion into a thriving business.

This guide is more than just a step-by-step manual; it's a companion for your entrepreneurial journey. We'll explore how to identify your niche, develop a business plan, secure funding, build a brand, create a strong online presence, and master the art of marketing. Each chapter is packed with practical advice, real-life examples, and actionable steps tailored to your needs as a mom and a budding entrepreneur.

But it doesn't stop there. As a mom, balancing your business with family life is crucial. I'll share strategies to manage your time effectively, maintain your motivation, and handle setbacks with grace. We'll also dive into the personal aspects of entrepreneurship, ensuring that you can achieve success without sacrificing your well-being or family time.

By the end of this guide, you'll have a clear plan, actionable steps, and the confidence to bring your business dream to life. You'll learn how to Conduct market research to understand your target audience and competitors, write a compelling business plan that outlines your vision and goals, Develop a unique brand identity that resonates with your customers, Build a user-friendly website and leverage social media to grow your audience, Implement effective marketing strategies to attract and retain customers, and Manage your finances and operations to ensure long-term success.

I wrote this book because I wish I had something like this years ago. My hope is that it empowers you on your journey, just as my dreams have empowered me. Remember, every successful business started with a dream. So, let's embark on this incredible journey together. Your dream is within reach, and I'm here to help you make it a reality. Let's get started!

Chapter 1: Dream Big, Mama!

Taking the Leap into Mompreneurship

So, why even start a business? For me, it was about freedom. Freedom to be there for my kids, freedom to chase my passion, and freedom to be my own boss. It's about turning those "what ifs" into "I did it!" moments. Plus, there's nothing like showing your kids that with hard work and faith, anything is possible.

Let me take you back to when I was 14 years old. I landed my first job as a cashier at a dollar store. Excited and ready to earn my own money, I walked in with high hopes. I had visions of independence, a little bit of cash in my pocket, and the pride of earning my keep.

I was nervous as hell. My hands were shaking, and I felt like everyone was watching, waiting for me to mess up. But even with all that anxiety, there was this fire in me. I knew that if I could just push through those jitters, I'd come out stronger on the other side. That first paycheck, no matter how small, was a taste of what it felt like to stand on my own two feet.

Unfortunately, my experience was a rude awakening. My training was a mere 60 minutes long, just a quick rundown of the register, the rules of the store, and a tour. No real guidance, no thorough explanation – just a "here you go" and a pat on the back. I was thrown into the deep end, and those nerves I felt? They were still very real. For the first three days, I was stocking shelves and cleaning up. But by day four, it was time for me to get on that register. It wasn't bad at all— at least, that's what I thought at the time. Little did I know, I was hitting the wrong function each time I had to remove an item from the customer's order. Instead of canceling it properly, I ended up cashing out the entire order and re-ringing the items, making it appear as two orders. By the end of my shift, my register came up short – extremely short. Not because I couldn't count money, but because of that honest mistake. I was devastated.

Despite my explanation, they let me go that very same day. I felt defeated, like the ground had been pulled out from under me. That feeling of being fired over a mistake was crushing. I knew right then and there, I never wanted to feel that way again. It opened my eyes to the reality that a job could fire me over a simple error, no matter how honest the mistake was.

That experience stuck with me all the way to today, especially when I started having children. I made a promise to myself that I would always have a backup plan because a job isn't real security. I learned over the years that solely relying on a paycheck from someone else could leave you out in the cold. So, I vowed to always have something on the side, something I built with my own two hands, to make sure my kids and I would be good no matter what. It planted the seed of wanting to be in control of my destiny, to create something where I wouldn't be at the mercy of someone else's decision.

Starting a business isn't just about making money; it's also about building something that belongs to me. It's about having the freedom to make mistakes, learn from them, and grow without the fear of getting fired, and being able to have something to pass down to my children it they wanted it.

Think about a time in your life when you felt the same. Maybe you were working a job that didn't appreciate your efforts, or perhaps you faced a situation where you felt powerless. How did it make you feel? Frustrated? Defeated? Eager for a change? Those feelings are powerful motivators. They push us to seek out new paths, to create our own opportunities, and to take control of our futures.

Starting my businesses has been my way of taking back control. I desire to build a life where I can be there for my kids and chase my passion without giving up my independence. I'm setting an example for my children, showing them that with hard work, perseverance, and a little faith, they can achieve their dreams too. But, I got to be real – it's not easy. You still may have to work a regular job while building the business, and that can be tough. Sometimes it feels like too much, and throwing in the towel on your dreams will seem like a better option. But is that an option you can live with for the rest of your life? There are days when I doubt myself, when things don't go as planned, and when I feel completely overwhelmed. It's in those moments that I have to dig deep and remind myself why I started this journey in the first place. These tough times are not just obstacles; they're opportunities for growth and learning. Every struggle is a lesson, every setback a chance to come back stronger.

As you read through this guide, I encourage you to keep that initial spark of your dream alive. Remember why you wanted to start a business in the first place. Whether it's for freedom, passion, or the desire to make a difference, hold on to that motivation. This journey won't always be easy, but it will be worth it.

Chapter 2: Finding Your Passion

One of the most important steps in starting your own business is finding your passion. This isn't just about picking something that sounds good; it's about finding what truly makes your heart sing and gets you out of bed every morning excited.

Finding your passion is the foundation of a successful and fulfilling business. It's what fuels your drive and keeps you going even when the going gets tough. Think about it: running a business isn't always a smooth ride. There will be challenges, late nights, and moments of doubt. But if you're doing something you're truly passionate about, those obstacles become easier to overcome because you're deeply connected to your work.

Passion brings a sense of purpose and direction. It's not just about making money; it's about creating something that resonates with your soul and has a positive impact on others. When you're passionate about what you do, it shows in your work. Your enthusiasm becomes infectious, attracting customers, clients, and partners who share your excitement and believe in your vision.

Moreover, passion is what sets you apart in a crowded market. It's the unique ingredient that infuses your business with authenticity and originality. When you're genuinely passionate about your product or service, you're more likely to go the extra mile to ensure its quality and success. This dedication can be the difference between a business that merely survives and one that thrives.

Finding your passion involves deep self-reflection. It's about understanding what activities make you lose track of time, what topics you can't stop talking about, and what brings you joy and fulfillment. It's about identifying your strengths and skills and seeing how they align with your interests. Sometimes, it requires revisiting childhood dreams and aspirations, as they often hold clues to your true passions.

Your passion should also align with your core values and beliefs. It's important to feel that your business is a true reflection of who you are and what you stand for. When your work aligns with your values, it creates a sense of harmony and balance in your life, making the journey more rewarding.

Finally, remember that finding your passion is an evolving process. It's okay to try different things and pivot when necessary. The journey of discovering what truly excites you can lead to unexpected and wonderful places. Be open to exploration and trust the process, knowing that each step brings you closer to finding the heart of your business. So, how do we find that magic? Let's break it down together.

First things first, take a minute to reflect on your interests. What activities make you lose track of time? What hobbies or topics do you keep coming back to? These interests can often point you towards your passion. Like, if you love cooking and experimenting with new recipes, maybe the culinary world is calling your name. Or if organizing makes you happy, a professional organizing service might be right up your alley.

Next, think about your strengths and skills. What are you naturally good at? What skills have you picked up over the years that come effortlessly to you? Our passions are often tied to our talents. For example, if you're a great communicator and love writing, maybe a blog or content creation business is your thing. Or, if you have an eye for design and love creating beautiful spaces, interior design might be your jam.

Now, let's take a little trip down memory lane. What did you love doing as a kid? Sometimes, our truest passions are hidden in those early dreams. When I was little, I dreamed about owning my own hair salon and doing hair for the stars. It seemed like a wild fantasy to my family, but dreaming big kept me wanting it anyway. That dream fueled my passion, kept me focused, and eventually led me down the path of entrepreneurship.

Think about what really drives you. What causes or issues are you passionate about? For some of us, our passion comes from a desire to make a difference. If you're all about environmental sustainability, maybe a business focused on eco-friendly products is your calling. If education is your thing, starting a tutoring service or an educational app could be the way to go. Knowing what drives you can help you create a business that aligns with your core values.

Finding your passion sometimes means trying new things. Don't be afraid to experiment and explore different interests. Volunteer, take up new hobbies, and immerse yourself in different environments. This exploration can reveal passions you never knew you had. And hey, it's perfectly okay to pivot and change directions as you learn more about what truly excites you.

In some cases, the people around us see our strengths and passions more clearly than we do. Talk to friends, family, and colleagues. Ask them what they think you're good at and what they see you being passionate about. Their insights can provide valuable perspectives and help you identify passions you might have overlooked.

Notice what activities energize you and make you feel alive. When you're passionate about something, it tends to energize you rather than drain you. If you feel invigorated after working on a particular project or talking about a specific topic, that's a good sign you've found something you're passionate about.

Your true passion can also be a combination of several interests and skills. For example, if you love fashion and have a passion for writing, starting a fashion blog or launching a fashion-related business that involves content creation could be your perfect fit. Don't be afraid to blend different passions and skills to create a unique business idea that excites you.

Take some time to visualize your ideal life. What does it look like? What kind of work are you doing? How are you spending your days? This exercise can help you gain clarity on what truly matters to you and what you are passionate about. Your ideal life is often a reflection of your deepest desires and passions.

Finding your passion is a journey, not a destination. It's a process of self-discovery that evolves over time. Be patient with yourself and enjoy the ride. Remember, it's never too late to find your passion and start a business that reflects who you are.

I'll share a story about a good friend of mine, let's just call her Jasmine. She was a go-getter, full of ambition and dreams, but like many, she was also driven by the desire for financial security. Jasmine had always been good with numbers and had a knack for spotting lucrative opportunities. So, when she heard about a booming trend in the tech industry, she jumped in headfirst, eager to cash in on the latest craze.

Jasmine invested her savings into developing a tech startup. It wasn't something she was passionate about, but she saw the potential for quick returns and the promise of financial freedom. For the first few months, things looked promising. Investors were interested, the media buzzed about her innovative idea, and money started flowing in. Jasmine was on cloud nine. She could already see the luxurious lifestyle she had always dreamed of a comfortable life for her and her two young children.

However, as time went on, the initial excitement began to wane. The tech industry was fast-paced and highly competitive. Keeping up with the latest trends required not just money but a deep, intrinsic passion that Jasmine simply didn't have. The initial influx of funds began to slow down, and the reality of running a business set in.

Jasmine soon encountered the inevitable slow months that come with any entrepreneurial venture. It was during these times that she found herself staring at her computer screen late at night, feeling the weight of uncertainty pressing down on her shoulders. The bills were piling up, and the revenue wasn't meeting her expectations. Her motivation, once fueled by the promise of quick success, started to slip away.

Every day was a battle to keep going. She had to constantly reassure her investors and her team, even when she wasn't sure herself. The slow months stretched into longer periods of uncertainty. She found herself second-guessing her decision. Why had she chosen something she wasn't passionate about? Why had she chased the money instead of following her heart?

With two kids depending on her, the pressure was immense. Jasmine would often lie awake at night, her mind racing with worries. How was she going to provide for her children if the business didn't pick up? What would happen if she couldn't make ends meet? The fear of failure was overwhelming. She remembered the stability of a regular paycheck, and for a moment, she longed for that security again.

Every day, she put on a brave face for her children. She didn't want them to see her struggle. But deep down, the doubt gnawed at her. Was she making the right choices? Could she really turn this around? The slow months tested her resolve, and the once-enthusiastic Jasmine found herself losing steam.

One particularly rough day, Jasmine found herself at her local coffee shop, staring blankly at her laptop. She overheard a conversation at the next table – a group of young women passionately discussing their startup ideas. Their excitement was palpable, and it struck a chord with Jasmine. They weren't just talking about making money; they were talking about creating something meaningful, something they loved.

It was a lightbulb moment for Jasmine. She realized that while she had been chasing money, she had neglected the most important element of success – passion. Without passion, her business felt like a chore, and every setback felt like a mountain.

Jasmine went home that night and did some serious soul-searching. She thought back to her younger days, to the things that had always made her happy. She remembered her love for fashion, her knack for styling, and how she always dreamed of creating her own fashion line. It seemed impractical at the time, but the passion was there, unlike her current venture.

She decided to pivot. It wasn't easy, and it meant starting over in many ways, but this time, she was driven by something deeper than money. She began working on her fashion line, pouring her heart and soul into every design. The slow months didn't disappear, but her perspective changed. The challenges were still there, but they felt different when she was working on something she loved.

Jasmine's story is a reminder that while chasing money might bring initial success, it's passion that sustains you through the tough times. Being an entrepreneur means facing uncertainty and slow months, but when you're driven by passion, those challenges become part of the journey, not just obstacles.

So, to all the moms out there juggling dreams and responsibilities, remember Jasmine's story. Follow your passion, because that's what will keep you going when the going gets tough. Passion fuels perseverance, and in the world of entrepreneurship, that's one of the keys to turning dreams into reality.

Chapter 3: Embracing Faith and Finding Purpose

Now that we've talked about passion, what I'm about to say might seem a little contradictory. Sometimes, pushing through your passion can lead to your true purpose. And let me tell you, only God can take you there.

Picture this: your passion is baking. You absolutely love everything about it – the feel of dough in your hands, the smell of fresh bread, the joy on people's faces when they taste your creations. Naturally, you dream of opening your own bakery. You imagine a cute little shop on a busy street, filled with the aroma of freshly baked goods. You see yourself behind the counter, greeting customers, and sharing your love for baking with the world.

Now, let's bring faith into the mix. You put your faith at the foundation of your dream, trusting that God will guide your steps. You work hard, save money, and finally, you open that bakery. It's everything you dreamed of, and you're overjoyed. But then, something unexpected happens. More and more young people start coming into your shop, not just to buy your bread, but to learn from you. They're fascinated by your skills and your story, and they want to know more. They ask if you can teach them how to bake.

At first, you're a bit taken aback. Teaching wasn't part of your original plan nor anything of interest. But you feel a nudge in your spirit, a gentle push from God saying, "This is where I need you." So, you start offering baking classes on the weekends. You teach these young people the art of baking, sharing your passion and skills with them. You see how it transforms their lives, giving them confidence and a sense of purpose.

Before you know it, your bakery becomes more than just a shop. It turns into a community hub, a place where young people come to learn, grow, and find hope. You realize that your true purpose is not just to bake, but to mentor and inspire the next generation. What started as a passion for baking has now evolved into something much greater – a mission to impact lives.

This is what I love about faith. It can change your path without warning, taking you to places you never imagined. When you put your faith at the foundation of your dreams, you open yourself up to God's plan for your life. Your passion might lead you to your purpose, but it's God who guides you there.

I've seen this happen time and time again, not just in my own life, but in the lives of so many others. Your initial passion might be the door that opens new opportunities, revealing new parts of yourself and stepping into who you are truly meant to be. And the best part? It can change at any moment.

Let's say your passion is fashion, and you dream of launching a clothing line. You work hard, design your pieces, and start your own brand. But along the way, you feel a pull to do more. Maybe you realize that the fashion industry needs more sustainable practices, and you decide to focus on eco-friendly clothing. Or perhaps you notice a lack of representation and decide to create a line that celebrates diversity and inclusivity. Your initial passion for fashion leads you to a greater purpose – to make a positive impact on the industry and the world.

Or maybe your passion is writing. You've always loved telling stories and dream of becoming an author. You write your first book, and it's a success. But then, you feel a call to use your gift in a different way. You start writing motivational books, sharing your journey and inspiring others to follow their dreams. Your passion for writing transforms into a purpose of uplifting and encouraging others.

The key is to stay open to God's guidance and trust that He has a plan for you. Even when things don't go as you expected, remember that God is working behind the scenes, orchestrating everything for your good. Your passion is the starting point, but your purpose is where you'll find true fulfillment.

So, keep pushing through your passion, but stay attuned to those gentle nudges from God. When you feel a shift, embrace it. It might take you out of your comfort zone, but that's where growth happens. Trust that God is leading you to something greater, something that aligns with His divine purpose for your life.

In my own journey, I've seen how faith can turn dreams into reality, often in ways I never imagined. It's a beautiful and sometimes surprising process, but it's always worth it. So, whatever your passion is – whether it's baking, fashion, writing, or something else entirely – know that with faith, you can go further than you ever dreamed. Trust in God's plan, and let Him guide you to your true purpose. It might not look like what you initially envisioned, but it will be exactly where you're meant to be.

Chapter 4: Overcoming self-doubt

I want to get personal and tackle something we all face: self-doubt. You know that nagging voice that creeps in when we're juggling motherhood, our changing bodies, and the constant worry of not being good enough? Yep, I've been there, and I'm here to share my journey to help you navigate those feelings.

When I became a mom, everything changed—my body, my routine, my priorities. It was easy to lose sight of who I was outside of being a mom. And when I decided to start a business, the pressure was real. I remember looking in the mirror, seeing the changes in my body, and thinking, "How can I possibly do this?" My weight became a constant source of insecurity. Society loves to make us compare ourselves to others, and I was no exception. The images of success around me didn't look like me, and that made me doubt myself even more.

I'd see other successful entrepreneurs and think, "I don't measure up." I felt like an imposter, constantly questioning my decisions and abilities. I wanted to be the perfect mom, the perfect partner, and the perfect entrepreneur. But let me tell you, perfection is a myth—it's an illusion that keeps us from moving forward. The first step in overcoming self-doubt is recognizing it for what it is: a normal part of the journey. It's okay to feel unsure sometimes. It's okay to question yourself. The key is not letting those doubts stop you.

One of the most freeing realizations I've had is that it's okay to be imperfect. Embracing imperfection is a strength because it means you're willing to grow, learn, and adapt. I used to think that my weight and appearance would hold me back. I thought people wouldn't take me seriously or like me because of how I looked. It was a toxic cycle that kept me from pursuing my dreams. But then I realized, it's not about how I look; it's about what I bring to the table. My ideas, my passion, my dedication—these are the things that matter. I started to focus on my strengths and what I could control. I embraced my imperfections and decided to show up authentically, just as I am.

Here are some strategies that have helped me, and I believe they can help you too. Let's dive into each one in detail.

First and foremost, it's okay to feel self-doubt. Acknowledge it, but don't let it control you. Understand that it's a part of the process, not a reflection of your worth. When those feelings creep in, take a moment to sit with them. Don't push them away or ignore them. Recognizing that you're feeling doubtful can actually help you understand why. Maybe it's a fear of failure, or perhaps it's the pressure of living up to certain expectations. By acknowledging these feelings, you can start to address them head-on rather than letting them fester and grow.

Remind yourself of what you're good at. It's easy to get caught up in what you think you lack, but focusing on your strengths can shift your mindset in a powerful way. Make a list of your accomplishments and skills. Keep it somewhere you can see it regularly. Whenever self-doubt creeps in, look at that list. Celebrate your wins, no matter how small they might seem. This practice helps build your confidence and reminds you of your capabilities. You are good at what you do, and you bring unique value to the table.

Building a support network of people who believe in you is crucial. Surround yourself with positive influences—friends, family, mentors, and fellow mompreneurs who can lift you up. It's important to have people in your corner who can offer encouragement and constructive feedback. They can remind you of your worth and potential when you're feeling low. Sometimes, just having someone to talk to can make all the difference. Don't be afraid to reach out and build those connections.

Taking care of yourself is crucial. Make time for activities that rejuvenate you. Whether it's a quiet bath, a walk in the park, or reading a good book, self-care is essential. It's easy to put yourself last when you're juggling multiple roles, but neglecting self-care can lead to burnout and increased self-doubt. Find what activities help you relax and make them a priority. Taking care of your physical, emotional, and mental health allows you to show up as your best self in all areas of your life.

Break your big dreams into smaller, manageable goals. This makes the journey less overwhelming and allows you to see your progress. Setting realistic goals helps you stay focused and motivated. It's important to be clear about what you want to achieve and set specific, measurable, attainable, relevant, and time-bound (SMART) goals. Celebrate each milestone you reach, no matter how small. Each step forward is progress, and acknowledging that progress can boost your confidence and reduce self-doubt.

Mistakes are not failures; they are lessons. Learn from them and use them to grow. Remember, every successful person has faced setbacks. It's part of the journey. When you make a mistake, take a moment to reflect on what went wrong and what you can do differently next time. Embrace a growth mindset—the belief that you can develop your abilities through hard work, good strategies, and input from others. Viewing challenges as opportunities to learn can help you overcome self-doubt and build resilience.

Picture yourself achieving your goals. Visualization can be a powerful tool to boost your confidence and keep you motivated. Take a few moments each day to imagine yourself succeeding. Visualize the steps you need to take to get there and see yourself overcoming obstacles. This practice can help you stay focused on your goals and reinforce your belief in your abilities. The more vividly you can imagine your success, the more real it becomes, and the more confident you'll feel in making it happen.

Lastly, be content with knowing that self-doubt will come and go. It's a part of the journey. The important thing is to keep moving forward. Embrace your imperfections, learn from your mistakes, and celebrate your progress. Remember, you're building an empire not just for yourself, but for your family. You're showing your kids that with hard work and faith, anything is possible.

Chapter 5: The Freedom 5

Alright, y'all, let's get down to business. Literally. Starting your own business is like being a kid in a candy store—so many possibilities, everything looks amazing. But before we dive into some business ideas that could be your ticket to freedom and fulfillment, let's talk about understanding the business behind your passion.

People love to say, "If it's something you love, be consistent and the money will come." That's cute, but it downplays the hard work and research necessary for building a successful business. Passion is the spark, but it's the planning, strategy, and grit that turn that spark into a thriving enterprise.

Which brings me to what I call The Freedom 5. These are the core areas where an entrepreneur generates profits: E-commerce Excellence, Service Savvy, Content Creation Mastery, Coaching Confidence, and Crafting Cashflow. Every entrepreneur aims to make an impact in at least one of these areas through their passion. Successful entrepreneurs maximize their passion in each area.

E-commerce Excellence Let's start with e-commerce. This is where my journey began. I had a passion for storytelling and writing, so I decided to sell my books online. Using platforms like Amazon, I set up my store and started selling. My gift of storytelling wasn't just limited to writing; I used it to market my books effectively, sharing the excitement and passion behind each story. The beauty of e-commerce is that you can start small with products you believe in and have tried yourself. Gradually, you expand as you see what your customers love.

Service Savvy From selling books, I ventured into providing services to other authors. I started Nu Class Publications, becoming the middleman who handled the financial backing and the legwork for authors who couldn't afford to publish on their own or didn't want to deal with the hassle. In what seemed like no time, my company grew to house over 27 authors. This wasn't just about making money; it was about using my skills and knowledge to help others achieve their dreams.

Content Creation Mastery From there, I expanded into content creation. I taught myself how to design high-quality book covers and other marketing items. Nu Class Graphicz was born. This part of my business grew on its own, and soon I was working with some of your favorite authors like K'wan, Thomas Long, Raquel Williams, and Lola Bandz, just to name a few. This is where social media came into play. As Instagram became the new hot topic, I started utilizing the platform, making videos of our pop-ups, conversations, how-to videos, and documenting our presence at popular book events. This was vlogging at its finest, creating awareness and building a community around my brand. I also had a Facebook group where I created premade covers and sold them a la carte for authors who didn't have the budget for custom designs. This allowed them to still get high-quality covers at a more affordable price.

Coaching Confidence My journey didn't stop there. I started teaching authors and aspiring graphic designers how to use Photoshop and create their own covers. This naturally fell into the coaching category. I realized that my experiences and the knowledge I had gained could help others navigate their own paths. Coaching became another branch of my business, where I could offer one-on-one sessions, group coaching, and online courses.

Crafting Cashflow The only area where my passion didn't quite fit was handmade goods. But that's okay because the other four areas were more than enough to create a thriving business. Nu Class Publications and Nu Class Graphicz did pretty well, consistently hitting five-figure months. This was all built on understanding my market, continuously learning, and adapting to new opportunities.

Now, let's talk research. Knowing your market is key. You need to understand who your customers are, what they want, and how you can solve their problems. This involves identifying your target audience, analyzing competitors, and understanding market trends.

My homegirl, Tanya, had a real passion for making candles. She was super creative when it came to candle scents and names. She spent countless hours perfecting her craft, and let me tell you, her candles were amazing. She had the best ads, a real gift of gab, and her product was genuinely good. Tanya was convinced she had everything she needed to be successful.

She set up her online store, posted beautiful pictures on social media, and even ran some paid ads. At first, there was some buzz, and she made a few sales. But soon, the sales started to slow down, and she couldn't figure out why. She had the passion, the quality product, and the marketing skills. What was she missing?

Tanya and I sat down one day and she shared her frustrations. As we talked, it became clear that Tanya hadn't identified her target audience. She was trying to sell her candles to everyone, without really knowing who "everyone" was. Her ads were too broad, her messaging was generic, and she didn't have a clear picture of who her ideal customer was.

We decided to dig a little deeper. We started by identifying who her potential customers could be. Were they young professionals looking for home decor? Busy moms needing a moment of relaxation? Gift shoppers looking for unique, handmade items? Once Tanya started narrowing down her audience, she realized that her main customers were people who loved self-care and relaxation products.

Next, we analyzed her competitors. We looked at what other candle makers were doing and found that many were targeting the same broad audience. But we noticed a gap: very few were focusing on the self-care niche. So, we decided to position Tanya's candles as the ultimate self-care accessory. We updated her branding, refined her messaging, and tailored her ads to speak directly to people who valued self-care.

We also looked at market trends. Self-care was a growing trend, and products related to relaxation and wellness were becoming increasingly popular. Tanya started creating content around self-care routines, sharing tips on how to create a relaxing environment, and even partnering with influencers in the wellness space.

The results were incredible. Tanya's sales picked up, and she started building a loyal customer base who loved her candles and resonated with her brand message. She learned that understanding her market was just as important as having a great product and good marketing skills.

So, what's the takeaway here? Research is necessary. You need to know who your customers are, what they want, and how you can uniquely serve them. Identifying your target audience helps you tailor your message and product to meet their needs. Analyzing your competitors helps you see what's already out there and how you can stand out. Understanding market trends keeps you ahead of the curve and ensures you're meeting current demands.

Don't just assume you know your market – take the time to research and understand it deeply. Tanya's story is a perfect example of how not identifying your audience can hurt your business, but also how turning that around can lead to success. If you have a passion, find out which of the Freedom 5 best fits your vision to make your passion profitable. And if you can put your passion into all five of these areas, you will surely scale and hit your business goals. Remember, research is your foundation. Build it strong, and your business will stand tall.

Chapter 6: Defining your brand

A brand is not just a logo or a catchy slogan. It's the essence of your business, the unique identity that sets you apart. A well-defined brand allows you to connect with your audience, build trust, and create a loyal customer base.

Why Defining Your Brand is Important

A well-defined brand helps you stay focused on your business goals. It keeps you aligned with your mission and values, ensuring that every decision supports your overall vision. This clarity helps both you and your team understand and embody your brand.

Consistency is key in branding. When your brand message is clear and consistent, it builds recognition and trust. People know what to expect from you, and that reliability is what keeps them coming back. Whether it's your social media posts, website, or customer service, everything should reflect your brand's identity.

Your brand is how you connect with your audience on an emotional level. It's about creating a feeling that resonates with them. When people feel a connection to your brand, they're more likely to become loyal customers. They'll choose your products or services because they identify with your values and your story.

Integrity in Your Brand

Integrity is at the heart of a strong brand. It's about being true to who you are and what you stand for, even when it's tempting to cut corners or take shortcuts. Let me share a personal story to illustrate this point.

When I first started writing, I was winging it. I had this burning passion and a story that needed to be told, but I didn't have a concrete plan. I rushed through the process, cutting so many corners. One major step I skipped was hiring a professional editor. I thought I could handle everything myself, and I was so eager to get my book out there that I didn't take the time to ensure it was polished.

When I released my first book, the readers chewed me up about how poorly written it was. The only thing that saved me was the storyline. It was a real page-turner, so people pushed through the horrible grammar, but that didn't stop them from letting me have it. I was stubborn at first. I didn't care about the criticism and kept my book on the market while I started working on my second novel.

But then, I attended a book fair in Harlem a few months after my release. I met the beautiful T. Styles and asked her for some advice. "How many times do you read your book to make sure there are no mistakes?" I asked. She removed her shades and looked me square in the eyes. "I have a team of editors. This is my brand we are talking about. I don't play about my name. You can lose 100 readers faster than you can gain them that way." Her words hit me hard. I felt so ashamed, unbeknownst to her. I couldn't wait to get home and pull my book off the market.

Even though I had a lot of people read the book with good feedback about the story, I started to think about all of the ones who stopped reading it and didn't provide feedback. They may never give me another chance. She was right; this was my brand—my name. If I was going to do this, I needed to put in 100% effort to make sure it was the best.

Skipping steps might seem like a shortcut, but it almost always leads to setbacks. Every part of the process, from editing to design to marketing, is crucial. Your brand is a reflection of you, and if you're not putting in the effort to make it the best it can be, it will show.

Building Your Brand

Defining your mission and values is essential. What do you stand for? What are your core beliefs and principles? Your mission and values should be at the heart of your brand. They guide your decisions and actions, ensuring that everything you do is aligned with your brand's identity.

Understanding your target audience is crucial. Who are you trying to reach? Know their needs, wants, and pain points. Speak their language and address their concerns. The more you know about your audience, the better you can tailor your brand to connect with them.

Crafting your story is a powerful tool. It's your chance to share your journey, your challenges, and your triumphs. A compelling story creates an emotional connection with your audience. Be authentic and honest. Share your struggles and how you overcame them. People love a good story, especially one they can relate to.

Creating a visual identity is also important. Your logo, color scheme, and typography are all part of your brand's visual identity. They should be consistent and reflect your brand's personality. Invest in professional design to ensure that your visuals are polished and cohesive.

Developing your brand's voice is crucial. How you communicate with your audience should be consistent across all platforms and materials. Whether you're writing a blog post, a social media update, or an email, your voice should reflect your brand's personality. Are you formal or casual? Playful or serious? Make sure your voice resonates with your audience.

Delivering on your promises is vital. Your brand is a promise to your customers. It's about delivering on what you say you will. If you promise quality, make sure your products or services meet that standard. If you promise excellent customer service, go above and beyond to ensure your customers are happy. Consistency in delivering on your promises builds trust and loyalty.

Evolving and adapting is necessary. Your brand isn't static. It should evolve as your business grows and as the market changes. Stay true to your core values, but be open to change and innovation. Keep an eye on trends and be willing to adapt to stay relevant.

Chapter 7: Setting SMART Goals

Let's dive into the nitty-gritty of setting goals—not just any goals, but SMART goals: Specific, Measurable, Attainable, Relevant, and Time-bound. Setting SMART goals is essential for running a successful business, especially when you're also juggling the beautiful chaos of motherhood. Let me break it down for you and explain why this matters.

The Importance of SMART Goals

Why are SMART goals important? Without a clear plan, you're just wandering aimlessly. You need direction, focus, and a way to measure your progress. And let's face it, with kids, time is a precious commodity. You can't afford to waste it on vague goals that lead nowhere. Setting SMART goals helps you prioritize, stay organized, and actually get things done.

The Chaos Without a Plan

Imagine you've decided to start a home-based bakery business. You've got your recipes perfected, and your friends rave about your cookies. But you didn't set clear goals. You thought, "I'll just bake and sell." Weeks go by, and you realize you haven't made any real sales. Why? Because you didn't set specific targets for how many sales you wanted each week or how you were going to market your products. You're baking your heart out, but it's not translating into profit.

Let's take another example. You're running a small online boutique. You're excited and ready to take on the world. But without SMART goals, you're working around the clock with no clear path. You're posting on social media at random times, trying different marketing strategies, and just hoping something sticks. Months later, you're exhausted, and your sales are inconsistent. You're spinning your wheels, and the lack of focus is draining you.

Both of these scenarios highlight the chaos that comes from not having a solid plan. It's like trying to drive to a new place without a map—you'll waste time, energy, and probably end up lost.

Implementing SMART Goals

So, how do you avoid this chaos? By setting SMART goals. Let's break down what that means:

- **Specific**: Your goals need to be clear and specific. Instead of saying, "I want to increase sales," say, "I want to increase sales by 20% over the next three months." This gives you a clear target to aim for.

- **Measurable**: Make sure your goals are measurable. You need to be able to track your progress. If your goal is to increase your social media following, specify how much. For example, "I want to gain 500 new Instagram followers in the next month."

- **Attainable**: Your goals should be realistic. It's great to aim high, but setting unattainable goals can set you up for failure and disappointment. If you're just starting out, don't aim to make a million dollars in your first year. Instead, set a more realistic goal that challenges you but is achievable.

- **Relevant**: Your goals should align with your business objectives. If your main aim is to build brand awareness, focus on goals that will help you achieve that, like increasing your social media presence or attending networking events.

- **Time-bound**: Set a timeframe for your goals. This helps create a sense of urgency and keeps you focused. Without a deadline, it's easy to procrastinate and push your goals aside. For instance, "I will launch my new product line by the end of the quarter."

Real-Life Application

When I first started my handbag brand, Lecce Capri, I was driven by passion and creativity. I had a vision of offering luxury handbag experiences at more accessible price points, especially for working moms. But in the beginning, I didn't set specific goals. I was all over the place, designing bags, reaching out to suppliers, and trying to market my brand without any clear direction.

One day, I decided to change that. I set a SMART goal: "I want to sell 100 handbags within the first six months of launching." This goal was specific, measurable, attainable, relevant, and time-bound. I broke it down further by setting monthly targets and outlining strategies to reach them. I focused on creating a strong social media presence, engaging with my target audience, and collaborating with influencers who resonated with my brand's values.

The results were incredible. By having a clear goal, I was able to measure my progress and adjust my strategies as needed. I reached out to mom bloggers and fashion influencers, offering them my bags to review and promote. I scheduled regular social media posts, created engaging content, and ran targeted ads. Slowly but surely, my sales started to climb, and by the end of the sixth month, I had sold over 120 handbags.

Setting SMART goals is not just a business strategy; it's a lifeline that keeps you focused and productive. Without them, you're likely to waste time and resources, and your efforts may not lead to the success you're aiming for. So, take the time to define your goals clearly, measure your progress, keep them attainable and relevant, and set a timeline. This will not only help you stay on track but also ensure that every step you take brings you closer to your ultimate business objectives.

Chapter 8: Me vs Time

One of the biggest challenges we face as mompreneurs: time. If you're anything like me, you probably feel like there are never enough hours in the day. Between managing the household, taking care of the kids, and trying to build a business, it's a constant battle to find time for everything.

The Mother's Busy Schedule

Let's take a look at a typical day for a mom. You wake up early, get the kids ready for school, make breakfast, and maybe even squeeze in a quick workout if you're lucky. Once the kids are off to school, it's time to tackle household chores—laundry, cleaning, and maybe running a few errands. Before you know it, it's lunchtime. The afternoon might involve more errands, preparing dinner, and then picking up the kids from school. After-school activities, homework help, and dinner prep follow, and by the time the kids are in bed, you're absolutely exhausted.

Now, where does building your business fit into all of this? It feels impossible, right? But here's the thing:

even if you can only devote 20 minutes a day to your business, that time adds up. Those small windows of time can help you check off items on your business to-do list and move you closer to your goals.

A Real-Life Application

When I first started building my handbag brand, Lecce Capri, I had to fit it into an already packed schedule. I would wake up an hour earlier to work on designs, send emails while waiting in the car for school pickup, and brainstorm marketing ideas while cooking dinner. It wasn't easy, and there were days when I felt overwhelmed. But by consistently dedicating small chunks of time to my business, I was able to launch and grow my brand. Life really got hectic when COVID-19 hit and they shut down in-person school. Suddenly, I was working from home, managing virtual school for the kids, and trying to figure out how to continue building a business in a world that seemed to only focus on essential items. It was overwhelming, to say the least. The house was always buzzing with activity, and finding uninterrupted time became even more challenging. But I knew I had to keep pushing forward, even if it was just a few minutes at a time.

Prioritizing Your Time

First, identify what absolutely must get done each day. These are your non-negotiables, like taking care of your kids, basic household chores, and self-care. Once you know your priorities, you can start to see where you might find those precious minutes for your business.

Writing down your daily schedule and looking for gaps can be incredibly helpful. Maybe it's during nap time, after the kids go to bed, or even while you're waiting in the car for school pickup. Even 20 minutes here and there can make a big difference.

Break your business tasks into small, manageable goals. Instead of trying to tackle everything at once, focus on what you can realistically accomplish in 20 minutes. It might be writing a quick email, planning your social media posts, or brainstorming ideas for your next project. These small steps will add up over time.

Using technology can also help manage your time more effectively. Calendar apps can schedule your day, set reminders for tasks, and keep track of deadlines. Tools like Trello or Asana can organize your to-do lists and prioritize tasks.

Don't be afraid to ask for help. Whether it's getting your partner to handle dinner one night a week or hiring a babysitter for a couple of hours, delegating tasks can free up more time for you to focus on your business.

Sometimes, you can combine business tasks with other activities. For example, listen to a business podcast while you're folding laundry, or brainstorm ideas while you're cooking dinner. Finding ways to multitask smartly can help you make the most of your time.

Consistency is key. Even if you can only find 20 minutes a day, stick with it. Those small windows of time will accumulate, and you'll start to see progress. It's about building momentum and making steady progress towards your goals.

Chapter 9: From Idea to Reality

First things first, you've got an idea. Great. But an idea alone isn't going to cut it. You need to develop it, flesh it out, and make it tangible. This means getting into the weeds of what your product or service is going to look like, how it's going to function, and why people are going to want it.

Think about it. Have you ever had a great idea that stayed just that—an idea? Let's change that. Grab a notebook and start sketching out your product or outlining your service. Get detailed. What are the key features? What makes it unique? This is where you brainstorm and refine. Don't rush this process. Your product needs to be rock solid.

Now, let's talk prototyping. This is where you create a sample or model of your product. If it's a physical item, make a prototype. If it's a service, outline the process and maybe run a trial version. The goal here is to see if your idea works in the real world. Even small steps count.

Next, we move to testing. Get your prototype or service in front of real people. Friends, family, anyone who can give you honest feedback. Listen to what they say. What works? What doesn't? Use this feedback to fine-tune your product or service. Think of someone you trust who could give you valuable feedback and reach out to them this week.

Creating the Business Plan

I know, I know, it sounds boring. But trust me, this is your roadmap to success. Without a plan, you're just wandering aimlessly. Now, I'll be honest with you—most small businesses don't start with a business plan. I was one of them. When I first started, I dove headfirst into my venture with nothing but passion and a vision. It wasn't until I was further into my entrepreneurial journey that I realized the importance of having a structured plan.

A business plan isn't just a formality; it's your guide. It helps you stay on course and measure your progress. Over time, I began creating a business plan and updating it each year. This practice has been invaluable, helping me refine my goals and strategies as my business grew and evolved.

Let's break it down.

Start with an executive summary. This is a snapshot of your business. Who are you? What are you offering? Why is it going to be successful? Keep it concise but compelling. This is your elevator pitch on paper.

Next, dive deeper into your business description. What problem are you solving? Who is your target market? What makes your business unique? Be clear and detailed. This is where you sell your vision.

Market analysis is crucial. You need to know who your competitors are and what the market looks like. Who are your customers? What are their needs and wants? How is the market trending? Use data and research to back up your points. This shows you know your stuff and are prepared to navigate the market.

Outline your business structure and team. Who's in charge of what? What roles are essential for your business to thrive? Even if it's just you right now, think about the future. Who will you need to bring on board as you grow?

Get into the details of your products and services. Describe what you're offering in detail. What are the benefits? How does it work? Why will people buy it? Be thorough and make it clear why your offering is valuable.

Your marketing and sales strategy is next. How are you going to attract and retain customers? What channels will you use to reach them? What's your unique selling proposition? This is where you outline your plan to get your product or service in front of the right people.

Finally, lay out your financial projections. This is where you detail your revenue goals and budget. How much money do you need to get started? How will you fund your business? When do you expect to break even or start turning a profit? Be realistic and back up your projections with data.

Here's a challenge for you: Set aside one hour this week to work on your business plan. Start with the executive summary and business description. Remember, you don't have to do it all at once. Break it down into manageable chunks. This plan will be your blueprint and, just like I do, you can update it each year (or sooner) to reflect your growth and new insights.

Time Management for Mompreneurs

Now, let's talk about the juggling act that is time management, especially when you're starting a business and raising kids. I've been through it all, and let me tell you, it's no joke. It's a constant balancing act, but I promise you, it's doable with the right approach.

After my divorce, I suffered from intense anxiety. When I get too overwhelmed, my body reacts in ways that are hard to ignore. My chest tightens, my head starts spinning—it gets bad. But practicing good time management has been a lifesaver for me. I made it a point to carve out time for my kids and myself, and let me tell you, prioritizing my time and sticking to a schedule has eliminated most of the chaos and unorganized mess from my life.

First things first, **create a schedule.** Block out specific times for work and family. Maybe you work early in the morning before the kids wake up or in the evening after they've gone to bed. Find what works for you and stick to it. It's all about finding your rhythm.

Set boundaries. When it's work time, focus on work. When it's family time, be fully present with your family. It's so easy to let the lines blur, but setting boundaries helps you stay focused and reduces stress. Trust me, it makes a world of difference.

Delegate and outsource. You don't have to do everything yourself. Hire help for your business tasks or get a babysitter for a few hours a week. Outsource tasks that aren't your strengths. If you're just starting off and can't afford to hire someone, look for ways to simplify and streamline your tasks. Focus on what you do best and find free or low-cost resources to help with the rest. For example, use free project management tools to stay organized or barter services with other moms who are in the same boat. Remember, it's okay to ask for help and lean on your community. Prioritize what's most important and tackle things one step at a time.

Use technology. There are tons of apps and tools out there designed to help you manage your time and stay organized. Use them. Whether it's a project management tool, a social media scheduler, or an accounting app, technology can be a huge time saver.

Self-care. Don't neglect yourself. Taking care of your physical and mental health is crucial. Make time for activities that rejuvenate you. Whether it's a workout, a hobby, or just some quiet time, self-care is essential for maintaining your energy and focus.

Here's another challenge for you: Create a weekly schedule. Block out time for work, family, and self-care. Stick to it for a week and see how it feels. Adjust as needed, but make sure you're setting aside time for each area of your life.

Chapter 10: Marketing Magic for Mompreneurs

Do you ever sit back and wonder how those big businesses keep growing their audience and retaining customers? It's not just about luck or having a massive marketing budget. It's about the magic behind the marketing—the strategy, the connection, and the consistency that make all the difference. Let's break it down and see how you can apply these principles to your own business.

Think about McDonald's and their Happy Meal. This wasn't just a product; it was a brilliant strategy. By offering a fun meal for kids, complete with a toy, they created an experience that kids loved and parents appreciated. It wasn't just about the food; it was about making meal times fun and memorable for families. This simple yet effective strategy singled out their product and created a loyal customer base that kept coming back.

Another great example is Planet Fitness with their "Judgment Free Zone" campaign. They understood that many people felt intimidated by traditional gyms. So, they created a safe, welcoming environment where everyone, regardless of their fitness level, could feel comfortable. This unique approach differentiated them from other gyms and attracted a whole new audience who might have otherwise stayed away from fitness centers.

So, how can you create your own magic behind the marketing? Let's get into it:

Understand your unique selling proposition (USP). What makes your product or service different from the rest? This is your magic. Whether it's a unique feature, a special experience, or a problem you solve better than anyone else, highlight it. Your USP is what will make you stand out in a crowded market.

Connect on a personal level. Don't just market your product; market your story. Share your journey, your challenges, and your triumphs. People connect with stories, not just products. Let them see the person behind the brand. This connection builds trust and loyalty.

Create an experience. Look at how Starbucks transformed a simple coffee purchase into a personalized experience. From remembering your name to customizing your drink exactly how you like it, they made every customer feel special. Think about how you can create a similar experience for your customers. Maybe it's through exceptional customer service, personalized touches, or creating a community around your brand.

Be consistent with your brand message. Consistency builds trust. Whether it's your social media posts, your email newsletters, or your customer service, make sure your brand message is clear and consistent. This helps create a reliable and trustworthy image.

Engage and listen to your audience. Social media is a goldmine for this. Don't just post content—engage with your followers. Reply to comments, ask for feedback, and really listen to what they have to say. This two-way communication makes your audience feel valued and heard, fostering a deeper connection.

Offer value beyond your product. Nike does this brilliantly with their Nike Training Club app, offering workouts, training plans, and health tips. They're not just selling shoes; they're offering a lifestyle. Think about what additional value you can provide to your audience that aligns with your brand.

Innovate and adapt. The market is always changing, and staying stagnant is not an option. Look at how Netflix transitioned from DVD rentals to streaming services. They saw where the market was headed and adapted. Stay ahead of trends and be willing to pivot when necessary.

Building an Online Presence

In the world we live in today, everything is accessible at the click of a button. It's no longer a luxury to have a strong online presence; it's a standard. If you want to make your mark and grow your business, you need to establish an online presence. This is your virtual storefront, where the magic happens. Think of it as setting up your shop, but instead of brick and mortar, it's all digital.

First off, **your website**. This is your home base, your digital headquarters. It's where people will learn about who you are, what you offer, and why they should choose you. Make sure it's clean, professional, and easy to navigate. Showcase your products or services, share your story, and make it easy for people to get in touch with you. Your website should reflect the essence of your brand and make a strong first impression.

Then there's **social media**. This is where you can really let your personality shine and connect with your audience on a personal level. Platforms like Instagram, Facebook, and Twitter are powerful tools for building your brand, engaging with your followers, and reaching new customers. Share behind-the-scenes looks at your business, celebrate your wins, and even share your challenges. Be authentic and let people see the real you.

Content creation is another key piece of the puzzle. Whether it's blog posts, videos, podcasts, or social media updates, content is how you provide value to your audience and keep them coming back for more. Share your expertise, offer tips and advice, and create content that resonates with your audience. This not only helps build your brand but also establishes you as an authority in your field.

Don't forget about **email marketing**. Building an email list is one of the most effective ways to stay connected with your audience. Send regular newsletters, updates, and exclusive offers to keep your subscribers engaged. Email marketing is a direct line to your audience and can be a powerful tool for driving sales and building loyalty.

And then there's **search engine optimization (SEO)**. This is how you make sure people can find you when they're searching online. Use relevant keywords, create valuable content, and optimize your website to improve your search engine rankings. The higher you rank, the more visible you are to potential customers.

Let's talk about **e-commerce platforms**. If you're selling products, platforms like Shopify, Wix, or even your own website's store can make it easy for customers to buy from you. Make sure your online store is user-friendly, with clear product descriptions, high-quality photos, and a smooth checkout process. The easier you make it for people to buy from you, the more sales you'll make.

Customer reviews and testimonials are gold. Encourage your happy customers to leave reviews and share their experiences. Positive reviews build trust and can be the deciding factor for new customers. Feature these testimonials on your website and social media to show potential customers that you're the real deal.

Keep this mental note, building an online presence isn't a one-time thing; it's an ongoing process. Stay active, keep engaging, and always look for new ways to connect with your audience. The digital world is constantly evolving, and staying on top of trends and technology will keep you ahead of the game.

One of the best perks of marketing for new mompreneurs is the magic of automation. In today's digital world, you can set up a lot of your marketing to run on autopilot, which frees up so much valuable time for your family and other business tasks. It's a real game-changer for us busy moms.

Take email marketing, for example. With tools like Mailchimp or ConvertKit, you can create automated email sequences to nurture leads, welcome new subscribers, and send out promotions. Once you've set it up, these emails go out automatically, so you're always in touch with your audience without having to manually send every single email.

Then there's social media scheduling. Apps like Buffer, Hootsuite, or Later let you plan and schedule your posts in advance. You can sit down once a week, create all your content, and schedule it to go out throughout the week. This way, your social media stays active and engaging, even when you're too busy to post in real time.

For managing customer relationships, tools like HubSpot or Salesforce are amazing. They automate follow-ups, manage customer information, and track interactions. This means you don't have to keep track of everything manually—your CRM does it for you, ensuring you stay on top of your customer relationships.

Chatbots and automated messaging systems, like ManyChat or Chatfuel, are also super helpful. They can handle customer inquiries, provide support, and guide potential customers through your sales funnel. These chatbots work 24/7, so your audience gets instant responses, even when you're not available.

Analytics and reporting tools like Google Analytics, Facebook Insights, or Sprout Social are also a big help. They generate automated reports and insights, tracking your marketing performance and giving you valuable data without the need for manual collection. This helps you understand what's working and where you can improve.

And if you're running ad campaigns, platforms like Facebook Ads and Google Ads are great because you can set them up to run automatically. You define your budget and target audience, and the platform optimizes your ads for you. This way, you can reach more people and get better results without having to constantly manage your campaigns.

The beauty of automation is that it allows your marketing to run smoothly in the background. It's like having a virtual assistant that works around the clock, keeping your brand visible and engaging without you having to be hands-on all the time.

For new mompreneurs, this is invaluable. It means you can scale your efforts, reach a broader audience, and grow your business without compromising precious family time. With apps handling much of the workload, you can manage your time more effectively and maintain a better work-life balance.

Content Marketing: Sharing Valuable Content

Sharing valuable content can resonate with your audience. It's all about giving before you get. Content marketing is a powerful tool that allows you to build trust, establish authority, and create a loyal following by offering something valuable to your audience without immediately asking for anything in return.

Understanding Your Audience: The first step in effective content marketing is understanding who your audience is and what they care about. What are their pain points? What are their interests? What kind of information or solutions are they looking for? By answering these questions, you can create content that truly resonates with them.

Blog Posts: One of the most common forms of content marketing is blogging. Let's say you run a small bakery. You could write blog posts sharing your favorite recipes, baking tips, or stories about how you started your business. This kind of content is valuable to your audience because it provides them with useful information and insights into your brand.

Videos: Video content is incredibly engaging and can be a great way to connect with your audience. For example, if you're a fitness coach, you could create workout videos, nutrition tips, or even live Q&A sessions where you answer fitness-related questions. This not only provides valuable content but also allows your audience to see and connect with you on a personal level.

Social Media: Platforms like Instagram, Facebook, and TikTok are perfect for sharing bite-sized content. If you're a fashion designer, you could share behind-the-scenes looks at your design process, styling tips, or sneak peeks of upcoming collections. This keeps your audience engaged and excited about what's coming next.

E-books and Guides: Offering free e-books or guides is a fantastic way to provide in-depth information on a topic your audience cares about. For instance, if you're a digital marketing expert, you could create an e-book on "10 Proven Strategies to Boost Your Social Media Presence." This not only showcases your expertise but also gives your audience valuable tools they can use.

Podcasts: Podcasts are a great way to share valuable content and connect with your audience on a deeper level. You could host a podcast where you interview experts in your field, share your own experiences, or discuss industry trends. This provides your audience with valuable insights and keeps them coming back for more.

Infographics: Infographics are a visually appealing way to present information. If you're a nutritionist, you could create infographics that break down complex nutritional information into easy-to-understand visuals. This makes your content more accessible and shareable.

Email Newsletters: Regular newsletters can keep your audience informed and engaged. Share tips, updates, and exclusive content with your subscribers. For example, a monthly newsletter from a travel agency could include travel tips, destination highlights, and special offers.

Webinars and Live Sessions: Hosting webinars or live sessions allows you to provide valuable information in real time. For example, if you're a business coach, you could host a live workshop on "How to Create a Business Plan." This interactive format allows your audience to ask questions and get immediate feedback.

Case Studies and Success Stories: Sharing real-life examples of how your product or service has helped others can be very powerful. If you're a software developer, you could write case studies showing how your software helped businesses increase efficiency or reduce costs.

User-Generated Content: Encourage your audience to create content related to your brand. For instance, a beauty brand could ask customers to share their makeup looks using a specific product and feature these on their social media pages. This not only provides valuable content but also fosters a sense of community and engagement.

By consistently sharing valuable content that resonates with your audience, you build trust and establish yourself as an authority in your field. People are more likely to engage with and support a brand that provides them with useful, interesting, and relevant information. Remember, it's about giving before you get—offering value without immediately asking for anything in return. This approach creates a strong foundation for a loyal and engaged audience.

Networking and Collaborations

the real talk about the power of networking and collaborations—essential moves for growing your business. It's all about who you know and who knows you.

First things first, join some mompreneur groups on Facebook, hit up local business events, and connect with other moms in your industry. These connections can lead to collabs, referrals, and some solid advice you can't get anywhere else.

Now, let's talk collaborations. Partnering with businesses that complement yours is a game-changer. Link up with a boutique clothing store and create exclusive baby clothing bundles. Do joint giveaways, create bundle deals, and shout each other out on social media. This way, you're expanding your reach and giving your customers more value.

Got a home-based baking business? Connect with a local mom who runs a party planning biz. Together, you can offer full party packages—cakes and treats from you, decorations and planning from her. This kind of collab not only expands your reach but also offers a comprehensive service that customers will love.

When it comes to sales strategies, it's not just about attracting customers but keeping them coming back.

Exceptional customer service is a must. Answer inquiries quickly, be friendly, and go the extra mile to make your customers happy. Happy customers turn into repeat customers and your biggest advocates.

Using promotions and discounts strategically can also make a big difference. Offer a first-time buyer discount to bring in new customers and run seasonal sales to boost revenue during slower months. Think about a loyalty program, too—reward your regulars with exclusive discounts, early access to new products, or special gifts.

Creating a sense of urgency is another smart move. Limited-time offers or limited-stock items push customers to buy sooner rather than later. Just keep it real—false urgency can backfire and kill trust.

If you've got an online store for eco-friendly baby products and see a dip in sales during the summer, run a "Summer Essentials" sale with discounts on season-appropriate items. Introduce a loyalty program where customers earn points for every purchase, redeemable for future discounts. These tactics attract new customers and keep your existing ones coming back.

Not every strategy is going to work for everyone or fit every business perfectly. What's important is playing around with all these strategies, tweaking them, and making them your own by adding your unique creative touches. That can be the secret sauce that sets your business apart.

Remember, each year might require a different strategy. What worked last year might need a refresh this year. That's the beauty of the game—always figuring it out, adapting, and finding new ways to keep things exciting and effective.

Maybe you'll find that collaborations give you a massive boost, or perhaps a loyalty program is what keeps your customers coming back. It's all about trial and error. Test different approaches, see what resonates with your audience, and don't be afraid to pivot if something isn't working as well as you hoped.

Stay flexible and keep your eyes open for new trends and opportunities. The business landscape is always changing, and the most successful entrepreneurs are those who embrace change and continuously seek out innovative solutions.

So, experiment, have fun with it, and don't get discouraged if something doesn't work right away. You're in this for the long haul, and every step, whether it's a success or a lesson learned, gets you closer to where you want to be.

Chapter 11: Scaling and Growing Your Business

When I kicked off Lecce Capri, the hype was real. Family and friends were buying my pieces and showing mad love. Sales were booming, and I felt like I was on top of the world. But as the buzz died down, reality hit hard. Orders slowed to a crawl, and my once-popping workspace was now a storage room for unsold inventory. It felt like I was stuck.

I found myself staring at piles of beautiful clothes that no one was buying. I wasn't hitting any of my sales goals, and I couldn't figure out why. It was frustrating and disheartening. I knew I had a great product, but something was missing. That's when it hit me – I hadn't done the proper research on how to grow and scale my business. I was so focused on getting my initial products out there that I forgot to think about the long-term strategy.

Introducing New Products or Services

First lesson learned: expand your product line. My initial collection was dope, but I needed to keep things fresh to attract new customers and keep existing ones interested. So, I started brainstorming new ideas. What else could I offer that would complement my clothing line and resonate with my customers?

I introduced our first luxury oversized fanny pack and new products like stylish accessories and matching mother-daughter t-shirts. My luxury oversized fanny packs were an absolute hit. Every time I restocked; they sold out almost immediately. That's when it hit me—I was excelling at marketing the luxury bags more than the apparel. After my fourth restock, I decided to add a matching mini messenger bag to the lineup. That was a hit as well, flying off the shelves just as quickly.

Seeing the success of these items made me realize the power of focusing on what my customers loved most. The variety of stylish accessories I introduced, including the fanny packs and mini messenger bags, breathed new life into Lecce Capri. Customers were excited and kept coming back to see what new items I had in store. This not only boosted my sales but also helped build a loyal customer base, eager for each new addition to the collection.

When and How to Bring in Additional Support

As Lecce Capri began to grow, I quickly realized I couldn't do it all on my own. There was only so much one person could handle, and trying to juggle everything was burning me out. It was time to bring in some help. This was a tough decision because, like many entrepreneurs, I felt like my business was my baby. Handing over parts of it to someone else felt daunting.

But hiring help doesn't mean losing control; it means freeing up your time to focus on the big picture. I started small by hiring a part-time assistant to handle customer inquiries and manage my social media. This allowed me to concentrate on designing new products and planning marketing strategies.

One of the best moves I made was surrounding myself with people who knew more than I did. Finding the right coaches and mentors was invaluable. They helped me learn and grow, offering insights and advice that I couldn't have gained on my own.

As your business grows, recognize when it's time to bring in additional support. Start with a part-time assistant or a freelancer to handle specific tasks like social media or customer service. This not only helps lighten your load but also brings in fresh perspectives and expertise.

As your business scales, consider bringing on more permanent team members. The key is to find people who share your passion and vision. Building a team of dedicated individuals allows you to focus on the strategic aspects of your business while they handle the day-to-day operations. With the right support system and mentors, you can drive your business forward and achieve your goals.

Staying Motivated

Growing a business isn't easy, and it's easy to get burned out. Keeping your passion alive is essential. There were times when I felt like giving up on Lecce

Capri. The excitement of starting my business had faded, and I was left with the hard grind of trying to keep it afloat.

Staying motivated requires a combination of self-care, goal-setting, and celebrating small wins. Take care of yourself – mentally, physically, and emotionally. Set realistic, achievable goals and celebrate when you hit them. Surround yourself with a supportive community, whether it's fellow mompreneurs, mentors, or family.

Remember why you started your business in the first place. Reconnect with that initial passion and let it drive you forward. It's not just about the end goal; it's about enjoying the journey and learning along the way.

Retaining Customers: The Secret Sauce to Growth

We often think that growing a business is all about getting new customers. While attracting new customers is important, retaining them is even more crucial. Treat your customers like kings and queens, making them feel valued and appreciated.

When I was stagnant in my business, I realized I hadn't put enough effort into retaining my customers. It's not just about making a sale; it's about creating a relationship. Personalized follow-ups, thank you notes, exclusive offers for repeat customers – these small gestures make a big difference. Happy customers not only come back but also spread the word about your business, doing the marketing for you through word of mouth.

Consider Sarah, a mompreneur who started a homemade organic skincare line. She knew her products were great, but what kept her customers coming back was her exceptional customer service. She remembered their preferences, sent personalized recommendations, and always made them feel special. Her customers felt valued and became her biggest advocates, helping her business grow through referrals.

Scaling and growing your business is a journey that requires careful planning, continuous effort, and a lot of passion. Expand your product line to keep things fresh, hire help to free up your time, use technology to streamline your operations, and stay motivated by remembering why you started. Most importantly, focus on retaining your customers. Treat them like royalty, and they'll not only come back but also bring their friends.

Chapter 12: Get Your Money Right

I'm glad to see you're still with me! Now, let's dive into something that took me years to learn: financial management. I'll be honest, when I first started out, I was winging it. As long as I saw the money coming in, I thought I was good. But running a successful business is more than just making sales; it's about knowing where every dollar goes and making your money work for you. And let me tell you, the dollars that go out can matter the most.

Budgeting and Cash Flow

I started Lecce Capri after having to close and liquidate Nu Class Publications due to the divorce decree. I used that money to start up another company because I just didn't have the mental capacity to go back to publishing after all the hard work that went into it. Using the money from one company to start another is not the norm because most people don't have money from a previous business to fund a new venture. This gave me the capital to buy inventory and get the business going. However, I ended up spending more than I anticipated due to poor financial management.

When I launched Lecce Capri, I was all about the hustle. I focused on making sales and keeping my customers happy. But behind the scenes, my financial management was a hot mess. I didn't have a clear budget, and my cash flow was all over the place. It took me years to realize that without a solid budget, I was flying blind.

Creating a budget is like setting the GPS for your business. It helps you see where you're going and how to get there. Start by listing all your income sources and expenses. Track everything — from supplies and marketing costs to rent and utilities. This will give you a clear picture of your cash flow and help you make informed decisions.

Think about it like this: if you don't know how much money is coming in and going out, you can't plan for growth. You can't invest in new products, hire help, or even pay yourself properly. A budget keeps you accountable and ensures that every dollar is working towards your business goals.

Setting the Right Prices for Your Products or Services

Setting the right prices for your products or services is crucial. When I first priced my Lecce Capri pieces, I was all over the place. I wanted to make them affordable for everyone, but I also needed to make a profit. It was a balancing act that I hadn't quite mastered. Realizing I needed help, I decided to hire a coach and enrolled in her twelve-week course on how to run an online boutique.

That was back in 2019, and it was one of the best decisions I ever made. The course covered everything from understanding my target market to setting competitive yet profitable prices. One of the most valuable lessons was structuring my pricing strategy to cover costs while ensuring a healthy profit margin. I also learned how to factor in all the hidden costs, like shipping and marketing, that I had previously overlooked.

The insights and practices from that course were incredibly valuable. I still use about eighty percent of what I learned from my coach today. Her guidance helped me refine my pricing strategy, streamline my operations, and ultimately build a more sustainable business. By implementing these practices, I found that sweet spot where my products were both appealing to customers and profitable for my business.

To set the right prices, you need to understand your costs and your market. Calculate the total cost of producing your product, including materials, labor, and overhead. Then, research your competitors and see what similar products are selling for. Finally, factor in the value you're offering and what your target market is willing to pay.

Pricing isn't just about covering your costs; it's about positioning your brand. Too low, and you might be seen as cheap or low-quality. Too high, and you might price yourself out of the market. Find that sweet spot where your prices reflect the value of your product and meet the expectations of your customers.

Here's a crucial lesson I learned the hard way: I didn't fully grasp the concept of knowing what a product cost me versus the profit I made until later in my business. I could have been losing money and didn't even know it because I didn't include the small things like packaging, taxes, or shipping costs. All these little expenses add up and can eat into your profit if you're not pricing correctly to see a real return.

Keeping Accurate Financial Records

Keeping accurate financial records is non-negotiable. You need to know exactly how much you're earning, spending, and saving. This isn't just for tax purposes – you must understand the financial health of your business.

Start by setting up a system for tracking your income and expenses. Use accounting software like QuickBooks or Xero, or even a simple spreadsheet if that's more your speed. Record every transaction, and reconcile your accounts regularly. This will help you spot any discrepancies and keep your finances in check.

Accurate bookkeeping also helps you identify trends and make data-driven decisions. You'll know which products are your best-sellers, where you're overspending, and where you can cut costs. It's all about having a clear picture of your financial situation so you can plan for the future.

Tax Planning: Understanding and Managing Your Tax Obligations

Taxes – the word alone can make anyone cringe. But understanding and managing your tax obligations is crucial for running a successful business. For years, I made sure my authors' tax documents were sorted, but when it came to my own business, I was often scrambling at the last minute.

The first step is knowing your tax obligations. Depending on your business structure, you may need to pay income tax, self-employment tax, sales tax, and more. Keep track of important deadlines and make sure you file your taxes on time to avoid penalties.

Consider working with a tax professional who can help you navigate the complexities of tax planning. They can offer advice on deductions, credits, and strategies to minimize your tax liability. And don't forget to set aside money for taxes throughout the year. It's tempting to reinvest every dollar back into your business, but you don't want to be caught off guard when tax season rolls around.

Financial management isn't the most glamorous part of being a mompreneur, but it's one of the most important. It took me years to learn the importance of keeping my books in order and understanding my true ROI. I was winging it for a long time, but once I got my finances in check, everything changed.

Remember, it's not just about seeing money come in; it's about knowing where every dollar goes and making it work for you. Create a budget, set the right prices, keep accurate records, and stay on top of your tax obligations. It might seem daunting at first, but trust me, it's worth it.

Understanding the true costs of your products, including the small details like packaging, taxes, and shipping, is essential. These hidden costs can quickly eat up your profits if you're not careful. Being diligent about your financial management will help ensure your business is not only successful but sustainable in the long run.

Chapter 13: The Heartbeat of Your Business

When you walk into a store, you want to feel welcomed and valued, right? Your customers deserve that same feeling, and it goes deeper than just a friendly smile. They should feel like they're stepping into a place where they genuinely matter, where their needs are the top priority, and where they're seen as individuals, not just transactions. Think about how you'd want to be treated – greeted with a warm smile, assisted with genuine care, and made to feel like you're the most important person in the room. That's the vibe you need to create for your business. It's more than just good manners; it's about building an experience that resonates with them on a personal level.

Outstanding customer service isn't just about being polite; it's about creating an experience that lingers long after they've left. It's about anticipating your customers' needs and exceeding their expectations. Whether it's answering questions promptly, offering personalized recommendations, or going the extra mile to solve a problem, it's all about making them feel valued and understood.

Let's say you're running a boutique clothing store. When a customer walks in, don't just let them wander around aimlessly. Greet them warmly, ask if they're looking for something specific, and offer suggestions based on their style and preferences. Make it personal. Remember their name, their likes and dislikes, and treat them like a VIP every time they walk through your door. Imagine the impact of saying, "Hi Tammy, we just got in a new collection I think you'll love," versus a generic greeting. That's how you turn a one-time shopper into a loyal customer who feels like they're part of your business family.

Your customers are the heartbeat of your business. Without them, your business wouldn't exist. They are the ones who keep the lights on and the doors open. They're not just numbers on a sales report; they're real people with real lives, and they choose to spend their hard-earned money with you. That's a big deal. By showing them that they matter, by going above and beyond to meet their needs, you're not just making a sale; you're building relationships. You're creating a community where your customers feel connected, appreciated, and eager to come back.

So, every time a customer walks through your door, remember: they are the reason you're in business. Treat them with the respect and care they deserve, and they'll reward you with their loyalty, their business, and their word-of-mouth recommendations. That's the true power of outstanding customer service – it turns everyday interactions into lasting connections.

Loyalty is the backbone of any successful business. Building a community of repeat customers who love and support your brand. Think about your favorite places to shop. Why do you keep going back? It's probably because you feel connected to the brand and valued as a customer.

To build that kind of loyalty, you need to create a sense of community. Engage with your customers on a personal level. Share your story, your passion, and let them see the real you. Use social media to connect with them, share behind-the-scenes content, and create a dialogue. Let them be a part of your journey.

Consider offering loyalty programs or exclusive perks for repeat customers. This not only incentivizes them to keep coming back but also makes them feel appreciated. For example, you could offer a discount after a certain number of purchases, early access to new products, or special events just for your loyal customers. It's all about making them feel like they're part of something special.

Think about how you'd feel if you received a personalized thank-you note with your order, or if the store you love gave you a discount just for being a loyal customer. You'd feel seen, valued, and connected. That's the kind of experience you want to create for your customers.

Handling Feedback and Complaints: Turning Negatives into Positives

No business is perfect, and there will be times when you receive negative feedback or complaints. It's how you handle these situations that can turn a potential disaster into an opportunity for growth. Let's be real – no one likes to hear that they've messed up, but facing criticism head-on is crucial.

First, listen to your customers. When someone has a complaint, they want to feel heard. Acknowledge their concerns, apologize sincerely, and take immediate steps to address the issue. This shows that you care about their experience and are committed to making things right.

Think about how you'd want to be treated if you had a bad experience in a store. You'd want someone to listen, understand your frustration, and make an effort to fix it. Do the same for your customers. Sometimes, turning a negative experience into a positive one can create an even stronger bond with your customer. They'll appreciate your honesty and effort to make things right.

Here's the deal: If a customer hits you up with a complaint about a defective product, don't ignore it. Reach out to them personally, apologize, and offer a replacement or a full refund. Maybe even throw in a discount code for their next purchase as a gesture of goodwill. Show them that you value their feedback and are willing to make things right. That customer will not only stick with you but also spread the word about how you handle your business.

Turning negatives into positives isn't just about damage control; it's about showing your customers that you value their feedback and are willing to learn and grow. It's about being transparent, taking responsibility, and making continuous improvements to your business.

Customer relationships are the heartbeat of your business. It took me years to fully grasp this, and I learned the hard way that you can't build a successful business without loyal customers. Sure, I made sure my paperwork was straight and sent out tax documents on time every year. But when it came to really knowing my overhead and the true ROI, I was winging it.

I didn't fully understand the importance of knowing what a product cost me versus the profit I made until later in my business. I could have been losing money and didn't even know it because I didn't include the small things like packaging, taxes, or shipping costs. All these little expenses add up and can eat into your profit if you're not pricing correctly to see a real return.

Chapter 14: Turning Struggles into Strengths

Let me ask you this, do you know the one thing every mompreneur has in common? If you say the drive, the motivation, or the vision... well, that's wrong. We don't always have those qualities. But no matter who the mompreneur is, or what business she started, she will in fact have setbacks. We all do! Running a business while balancing life, family, and everything in between isn't a walk in the park. It's more like a marathon with hurdles. But here's the deal: every setback, every stressful day, every moment of doubt is an opportunity to grow stronger and smarter. Let's break it down and talk about how to overcome these challenges, because I've been there, and I know you can too.

Dealing with Setbacks: How I Bounced Back from Failures and Mistakes

We all mess up. We all face setbacks. It's part of the game. But what separates successful entrepreneurs from the rest is the ability to bounce back. There were times when I felt like giving up because things weren't going as planned. But here's the thing – every failure taught me something valuable. Each setback was a lesson in disguise.

When I first started Lecce Capri, I made plenty of mistakes. Sometimes, I launched products that didn't sell as expected or made bad financial decisions. I was spending money I didn't even have. Almost to the point where I was robbing Peter to pay Paul for my house bills. There were times I spent thousands of dollars on a product that I couldn't sale due to defects. Can you imagine looking at a stack of boxes full of inventory that you can't sale. It was money down the drain. I felt defeated, but I had to learn to acknowledge my mistakes. I owned up to them and figured out what went wrong. I had to analyze and learn from each situation to make better decisions next time. Staying positive was crucial – setbacks are temporary. I kept my eyes on my goals and took action to correct my course.

Let me keep it real with you – staying positive when life throws everything at you can be tough. I had my moments where it felt like the weight of the world was on my shoulders. But I took it day by day, knowing that each small step forward was progress.

I spent hours watching motivational videos from powerhouses like Eric Thomas, Sarah Jakes Roberts, and Myron Golden. Their words weren't just uplifting; they were lifelines. Eric Thomas's fire, Sarah Jakes Roberts' wisdom, and Myron Golden's insights hit home in a way that made me feel seen and understood. They reminded me that I wasn't alone in my struggles, and their messages gave me the strength to keep pushing forward.

But it wasn't just about the videos. I prayed – a lot. I sought guidance and found solace in my faith. There were nights where I felt overwhelmed, but those prayers were my conversations with God, where I poured out my fears and doubts. And slowly, those conversations turned into a source of strength and clarity.

It was a struggle to stay positive, and there were days when I wondered if I could keep going. But each day, I made the choice to get back up, to find a little bit of light even in the darkest times. This combination of motivational speakers, prayer, and sheer determination helped me bounce back stronger than ever.

Taking it one day at a time, I learned that resilience isn't about never falling; it's about always getting back up. And with every step, I grew stronger, wiser, and more determined to keep pushing toward my dreams.

Work-Life Balance: Tips and Strategies for Managing Stress and Maintaining Balance

Let's be real – balancing work and life is no joke, especially when you're running a business and taking care of a family. It's easy to feel overwhelmed and stressed out. But keeping a healthy work-life balance is crucial for your sanity and your success.

Here are some tips that helped me manage stress and maintain balance:

1. **Set Boundaries**: I had to draw clear lines between work time and family time. When I was with my family, I made it a point to be fully

present. Shutting off work mode and focusing on my loved ones was essential for me.

2. **Create a Schedule**: Planning out my day and sticking to it kept me organized. Having a schedule ensured I carved out time for both work and family, making sure neither got neglected.

3. **Take Breaks**: I learned the hard way that taking breaks during my workday is crucial. Even a short walk or a quick meditation session helped me recharge and reduce stress.

4. **Ask for Help**: I wasn't afraid to ask for help when I needed it. Whether it was hiring a babysitter or asking a friend to watch the kids for a few hours, I learned it's okay to lean on others.

Finding balance wasn't about being perfect; it was about making conscious choices that prioritized my well-being and my family's needs. It's a daily commitment to managing stress and ensuring that both my business and my family get the best version of me. So, if you're feeling overwhelmed, remember that it's okay to ask for help, take breaks, and set boundaries. We've got this, one day at a time.

Health and Wellness: Taking Care of Myself While Running a Business

Your health and wellness are non-negotiable. You can't pour from an empty cup, and if you're not taking care of yourself, your business and your family will suffer. Trust me, I've learned this the hard way.

Here's how I stayed healthy and well while running my business:

1. **Prioritize Self-Care:** I made time for myself every day, even if it was just 15 minutes. Whether it was reading a book, taking a bath, or going for a run, I did something that made me feel good.

2. **Eat Well:** Fueling my body with nutritious foods was essential. It was easy to grab fast food when I was busy, but healthy meals kept me energized and focused.

3. **Stay Active:** I incorporated physical activity into my routine. Exercise reduced stress and boosted my mood. I found activities I enjoyed, whether it was yoga, dancing, or hitting the gym.

4. **Get Enough Sleep:** I didn't sacrifice sleep for work. Aiming for at least 7-8 hours of sleep each night made me more productive and creative.

Taking care of myself wasn't selfish; it was necessary. My health was my most valuable asset, so I treated it with the importance it deserved.

Continual Learning: Staying Updated and Continually Improving My Skills

The business world is constantly evolving, and to stay ahead, you need to keep learning and improving your skills. It's easy to get comfortable, but growth happens outside your comfort zone.

Here's how I stayed updated and continually improved:

1. **Read Books and Articles:** I kept up with industry trends and best practices by reading books,

blogs, and articles. Knowledge is power, and the more I knew, the better I was at navigating my business.

2. **Take Courses and Workshops:** Investing in my education by taking courses and attending workshops kept me sharp and competitive. Whether it was learning a new marketing strategy or mastering a software tool, continual learning was crucial.

3. **Network with Peers:** I connected with other entrepreneurs and industry experts. Networking opened doors to new opportunities and provided valuable insights and support.

4. **Seek Feedback:** I wasn't afraid to ask for feedback from my customers, peers, and mentors. Constructive criticism helped me improve and grow.

Learning was a lifelong journey, and the more I invested in myself, the more I saw my business thrive.

Overcoming challenges is all about mindset and action. It's about acknowledging setbacks, learning from them, and bouncing back stronger. It's about finding balance in your work and personal life, taking care of your health, and continually improving your skills.

Remember, every challenge is an opportunity to grow. Embrace the struggles, learn from them, and keep pushing forward. You've got the strength, the hustle, and the resilience to turn every obstacle into a steppingstone toward success. So, let's tackle these challenges head-on and build a business that thrives, no matter what comes our way.

Chapter 15: Building a Legacy

Let's talk about building a legacy, something that goes beyond just making ends meet. Growing up, I watched my family live paycheck to paycheck. My parents worked tirelessly to ensure I had a normal childhood, shielding me from the financial struggles they faced. It wasn't until I got older that I realized how hard they worked to keep our heads above water. They gave their all, but without any real ownership or assets, there was nothing substantial to pass down. They worked their whole lives, and yet, they had nothing to show for it in the end. That's a cycle I'm determined to break.

Building my business isn't just about success in the here and now; it's about creating generational wealth. It's about making sure my children, and their children, have a solid foundation to build on. Generational wealth means passing down assets, not just memories. It means giving the next generation a head start, something many of us in the Black community have been denied for far too long.

Tammy Capri

In our community, the importance of generational wealth cannot be overstated. For too many of us, financial instability is a norm passed down through generations. We've seen our families work their entire lives, only to end up with little to show for it but hard-earned lessons. This cycle of living paycheck to paycheck, of working without ever truly owning, is something I'm committed to ending. I want to be the one to break those generational curses and create a legacy of prosperity and opportunity.

I want my children to inherit more than just debt and hard times. I want them to have the financial freedom to pursue their dreams without the heavy burden of financial insecurity. By building a successful business, I'm laying the groundwork for that legacy. I'm creating something that can be passed down, something that will provide for my family long after I'm gone. It's not just about the money; it's about the security, the opportunities, and the peace of mind that come with it.

When I look at my parents, I see their hard work, their sacrifices, and their love. But I also see the gaps – the lack of ownership, the absence of generational wealth. I don't want my children to look back and see those same gaps. I want them to see a legacy of strength, resilience, and prosperity. I want them to know that their mom didn't just work to survive, but to build a future they could thrive in. That's what building a legacy is all about – creating a better tomorrow, today.

Reflecting on my childhood, I remember the constant stress of financial uncertainty. My parents did their best to shield me from it, but as I grew older, the reality became clear. They worked incredibly hard, often juggling multiple jobs, just to make sure we had a roof over our heads and food on the table. Their sacrifices were immense, but despite their efforts, we had no real wealth to show for it. No savings, no investments, nothing that could be passed down to ease the burden on the next generation.

This realization hit me hard. I understood that if I didn't do something different, I would be passing the same struggles down to my children. The thought of my kids facing the same financial hurdles I did was unbearable. I knew I had to find a way to create lasting change – not just for me, but for my entire family. This is where the concept of generational wealth became my driving force.

Generational wealth isn't just about accumulating money. It's about creating assets that appreciate over time and can be passed down to future generations. It's about owning property, building a business, investing in education, and creating a financial safety net that ensures stability and growth for years to come. For the Black community, this is particularly important. Historically, we've been excluded from many opportunities that foster generational wealth, such as home ownership and access to quality education. It's time to change that narrative.

Starting my business was a leap of faith, but it was also a strategic move towards building that legacy. I wanted to create something that not only provided for my family now but would also stand the test of time. My business is more than a source of income; it's an investment in our future. Every decision I make is with the intention of building something sustainable and impactful. This means thinking long-term, making smart financial choices, and always looking for ways to grow and expand.

One of the key aspects of building generational wealth is financial literacy. Understanding how money works, how to save, invest, and manage it effectively is crucial. This is knowledge I'm committed to passing down to my children. I want them to understand the value of a dollar, but more importantly, I want them to understand the power of money as a tool for building wealth. This involves teaching them about budgeting, investing in stocks and real estate, and the importance of having multiple streams of income.

Another important aspect is ownership. Owning property and businesses are fundamental steps towards financial independence and wealth creation. I'm focused on acquiring assets that can be passed down, such as real estate and stocks. These are not just investments for me; they are investments for my children and their future families. Each property purchased, each stock acquired, is a building block in the foundation of our family's financial security.

I also believe in the power of community and networking. Building a legacy isn't something you do in isolation. It's about creating connections, finding mentors, and helping others along the way. I've been blessed with a supportive network of like-minded individuals who are also focused on creating generational wealth. We share knowledge, resources, and opportunities, lifting each other up as we climb. This sense of community is vital, especially in the Black community, where collective progress can lead to significant change.

Education is another pillar of generational wealth. Ensuring my children have access to quality education is non-negotiable. This doesn't just mean formal education, but also teaching them practical skills and knowledge that will help them thrive in the real world. Whether it's learning about finance, entrepreneurship, or developing a strong work ethic, education is the key to unlocking opportunities and achieving long-term success.

Building a legacy also means preparing for the future. This involves having a solid financial plan, including life insurance, retirement accounts, and a will. These are often overlooked, but they are essential components of ensuring that your wealth is protected and passed down efficiently. I'm dedicated to setting up these structures now so that my family is taken care of, no matter what.

Ultimately, building a legacy is about more than just financial stability. It's about creating a lasting impact that will benefit generations to come. It's about breaking the cycle of poverty and struggle, and replacing it with a cycle of prosperity and opportunity. It's about ensuring that my children, and their children, have the resources they need to live fulfilling lives, pursue their dreams, and contribute to society in meaningful ways.

When I think about the future, I see a family that's not just surviving, but thriving. I see my children confident and empowered, with the knowledge and resources to navigate the world and achieve their goals.

I see them passing down these values and resources to their own children, continuing the legacy of strength and resilience. This vision is what drives me every day. It's what keeps me pushing forward, even when the road gets tough.

Building a legacy is a journey, and it's one that requires dedication, perseverance, and a clear vision. It's about making conscious choices every day that align with your long-term goals. It's about staying focused and committed, even when faced with challenges. And most importantly, it's about believing in your ability to create change and build something lasting.

For anyone on this journey, remember that you have the power to shape your future. Every decision you make, every step you take, is a part of your legacy. Stay focused, stay determined, and never lose sight of your vision. Together, we can create a future where generational wealth is the norm, not the exception. We can build legacies that will stand the test of time, leaving a lasting impact on our families and communities for generations to come.

Final Chapter: Embrace Your Journey & Trust in God

As we close this chapter together, I want to leave you with some final thoughts and reflections on the journey you're about to undertake. Building a business is not just about strategies and tactics; it's about heart, faith, and resilience. It's about embracing the unique path that God has laid out for you and trusting in His guidance every step of the way.

When I started my journey, I had no idea where it would lead me. All I knew was that I had a vision and a burning desire to create something meaningful. Along the way, I faced countless obstacles, moments of doubt, and times when giving up seemed like the easiest option. But through it all, my faith in God kept me grounded. I prayed, I listened, and I trusted that He had a plan for me, even when I couldn't see it myself.

One of the most important lessons I've learned is that everyone's journey is different. The road you're on may have twists and turns, ups and downs, but that's what makes it uniquely yours. There is no one-size-fits-all formula for success. The tips and insights I've shared in this book are based on my experiences, but it's up to you to find the best path for your journey. Embrace the beauty of your unique road, and never be afraid to forge your own path.

God has a way of putting us exactly where we need to be, even if it doesn't always make sense at the time. There were moments in my journey when I questioned why certain things were happening. Why was I facing so many challenges? Why did success seem so far out of reach? But looking back, I can see that every setback was a setup for something greater. Every challenge was an opportunity for growth, and every closed door led me to a new and better one.

As you move forward, remember to keep God at the center of your journey. Pray for guidance, seek His wisdom, and trust that He is leading you towards your purpose. There will be times when you feel lost or unsure, but that's when you need to lean into your faith the most. God's plan for you is greater than anything you can imagine, and He will provide the strength and clarity you need to keep moving forward.

One of the keys to a successful and fulfilling journey is to never stop enjoying the ride. It's easy to get caught up in the hustle and bustle of building a business, but don't forget to take a step back and appreciate the journey itself. Celebrate your victories, no matter how small. Learn from your failures, and use them as stepping stones to greater success. Surround yourself with people who lift you up and support your dreams. And most importantly, find joy in the process.

Building a business is hard work, but it's also incredibly rewarding. There's nothing quite like the feeling of seeing your vision come to life, knowing that you've created something that makes a difference. But it's important to remember that success is not just about reaching the destination; it's about the journey. It's about the lessons you learn, the relationships you build, and the person you become along the way.

As you embark on your own journey, keep these principles in mind:

1. **Stay True to Yourself**: Authenticity is your greatest asset. Be true to who you are, and let your unique voice shine through in everything you do. Your authenticity will attract the right people and opportunities to your business.

2. **Trust the Process**: Building a business takes time, and there will be moments of doubt and uncertainty. Trust the process, and have faith that everything is unfolding as it should. Remember, God's timing is always perfect.

3. **Embrace the Challenges**: Every challenge you face is an opportunity for growth. Embrace them, learn from them, and use them to become stronger and wiser. Don't be afraid to step out of your comfort zone and take risks. That's where the magic happens.

4. **Seek Guidance and Support**: You don't have to do it alone. Seek guidance from mentors, surround yourself with a supportive community, and don't be afraid to ask for help. Collaboration and connection are key to success.

5. **Celebrate Your Wins**: Take the time to celebrate your achievements, no matter how small. Recognize the progress you've made and appreciate the journey. Celebrating your wins will keep you motivated and remind you of how far you've come.

6. **Keep God at the Center**: Your faith is your anchor. Keep God at the center of your journey, and trust in His plan for you. Pray for guidance, seek His wisdom, and let His love and light guide you every step of the way.

As we wrap up this book, I want to remind you that your journey is uniquely yours. Embrace it with all its beauty, challenges, and triumphs. Trust in God's plan, and never lose sight of your dreams. You have everything you need within you to succeed. Believe in yourself, stay committed to your vision, and keep moving forward with faith and determination.

Remember, this is just the beginning. Your story is still being written, and the best is yet to come. Keep pushing, keep striving, and never stop believing in the incredible power within you. You are capable of achieving greatness, and your journey is a testament to that.

Thank you for allowing me to share my journey with you. I hope my experiences, insights, and faith have inspired you to embark on your own path with confidence and courage. May God bless you abundantly as you pursue your dreams, and may your journey be filled with joy, growth, and endless possibilities.

Here's to building a legacy, creating generational wealth, and making a lasting impact. The road ahead may be challenging, but it's also filled with endless opportunities. Embrace the journey, trust in God, and never stop enjoying the ride. You've got this, and I can't wait to see the incredible things you will achieve.

Connect with Tammy Capri

Thank you for joining me on this journey through **Business Beginnings**. Your support and engagement mean the world to me. If you'd like to stay connected, share your own entrepreneurial stories, or simply follow along for more inspiration and updates, here are the best ways to connect with me:

Follow Me on Instagram

Stay up-to-date with my latest projects, behind-the-scenes moments, and daily motivation by following me on Instagram: @tammycapri_

Join The Boss Mom Huddle

Looking for a community of like-minded mompreneurs? Join **The Boss Mom Huddle** for resources, support, and empowerment: www.TheBossMomHuddle.com

Explore Lecce Capri

Discover our luxury handbag collection designed for the modern, empowered woman. Explore our products and find the perfect piece to complement your style: www.LecceCapri.com

www.ingramcontent.com/pod-product-compliance
Lightning Source LLC
Chambersburg PA
CBHW071930210526
45479CB00002B/616